Mental Health and Wellness

Franklin Fisher

Copyright © (2024) by Franklin Fisher

All rights reserved. No portion of this book may be reproduced, stored, in a retrieval system or transmitted in any format or by any means, electronical, mechanical, photocopying, recording, or otherwise, without the prior written permission of the author.

Published by Amazon KDP

Amazon.com, Inc.

P.O. Box 81226

Seattle, WA 98108-1226

United States.

Printed by Amazon KDP in the USA

Table of Contents

Chapter 1
Introduction to Mental Health

Overview of Mental Health

Our entire well-being, which includes our emotional, psychological, and social states of being, is largely dependent on our mental health. It includes both the absence of mental disease and the existence of beneficial traits like emotional control, resilience, and self-worth. It's critical to acknowledge the significance of mental health in order to lead happy and fruitful lives, just as we prioritize physical health.

The Significance of Mental Health

Every element of our lives is impacted by our mental health, including our thoughts, feelings, social interactions, and stress management. Prioritizing mental health improves our capacity to handle life's obstacles, build deep connections, and follow our passions.

Investigating Mental Illness

Mental illnesses are medical problems that cause disturbances in an individual's thoughts, emotions, behavior, mood, or capacity to manage day-to-day activities. They can include less severe ailments like anxiety and sadness or more serious ones like bipolar illness and schizophrenia. It's critical to realize that mental diseases are complicated disorders brought on by a confluence of biological, psychological, environmental, and genetic elements rather than being defects in personality or personal failings.

Frequently Held Myths Regarding Mental Health

Regrettably, there are a lot of false beliefs about mental health that can support stigma and discourage people from getting the care they need. Among the widespread misunderstandings are:

1. Mental illness is not common: In actuality, millions of individuals worldwide suffer from mental diseases, which are extremely frequent. One in four people will at some point in their lives have a mental health issue, according to the World Health Organization.

2. The misconception that mental disorders are a sign of weakness challenges the fact that mental illnesses are medical conditions that need to be treated, much like any

other ailment. Seeking assistance for mental health issues is not a show of weakness but rather of strength.

3. Individuals suffering from mental illness are hazardous or violent: Most persons suffering from mental illness are not violent. It is much more likely for them to be the victims of violence than the offenders. Mental illness does not characterize or dictate a person's actions.

4. You can "snap out of it": People with mental illnesses cannot "will" themselves better; they are not choices. It's common for recovery to involve medical care, family support, and self-care techniques.

Useful Advice for Promoting Mental Health

1. Make self-care a priority: Schedule time for things like exercise, meditation, hobbies, and quality time with loved ones that benefit your mind, body, and spirit.

2. Engage in mindfulness exercises: Develop a judgment-free present-moment awareness of your thoughts, feelings, and sensations. Stress levels can drop and general wellbeing can rise with mindfulness.

3. Seek assistance: If you're having trouble, don't be afraid to get in touch with friends, family, or mental health specialists. You don't have to confront difficulties by yourself.

4. Become informed: Get more knowledge about mental health, including common problems,

available treatments, and coping mechanisms. You can speak up for others and yourself when you are well-informed.

Sources for Additional Research

- National Alliance on Mental Illness (NAMI): Offers advocacy, information, and support to those who are impacted by mental illness.

- MentalHealth.gov: Provides information and instruments to support mental health and facilitate treatment access.

- Apps for therapy: Look into smartphone apps such as Calm, BetterHelp, and Talkspace to get easy access to resources for mental health and treatment.

- Local support groups: Search for internet forums or community-based support groups where you can get in touch with people going through comparable struggles.

We can promote a climate of acceptance, support, and resilience by educating others about mental health, clearing up myths, and emphasizing the importance of taking care of ourselves.

Chapter 2
The Mind-Body Connection

Investigating the complex connection between physical and emotional health

The relationship between our mental and physical health, emphasizing how one can affect the other, is known as the "mind-body connection." Maintaining general wellbeing and successfully addressing issues related to mental and physical health depend on an understanding of this link.

The Relationship Between Physical and Mental Well-Being

Empirical studies have demonstrated the tight relationship between mental and physical well-being. For instance, long-term stress can impair immunity, increasing a person's susceptibility to disease. On the other hand, physical conditions like persistent pain can have a substantial effect on mental health and cause symptoms of worry and despair. Achieving holistic wellbeing requires an understanding of the interactions between mental and physical health and taking appropriate action.

The Effects of Lifestyle Decisions on Mental Health

1. **Exercise:** Research has demonstrated that regular physical activity has a number of positive effects on mental health, including lowering anxiety and depressive symptoms, elevating mood, and boosting general wellbeing. Most days of the week, try to get in at least 30 minutes of moderate exercise, including brisk walking, cycling, or swimming.

2. **Nutrition:** For both physical and mental well-being, a balanced diet full of fruits, vegetables, whole grains, lean meats, and healthy fats is necessary. There is evidence linking some nutrients, like folate and omega-3 fatty acids, to enhanced mood and cognitive performance. Processed meals, sugary snacks, and caffeine should be avoided in excess as they can have a detrimental effect on mood and energy levels.

3. **Sleep:** Since it enables the brain to regenerate and mend itself, getting enough sleep is essential for mental health. Set up a regular sleep pattern and try to get between seven and nine hours of sleep every night. Establish a peaceful nighttime routine, avoid using electronics just before bed, and

create a cozy sleeping space to practice excellent sleep hygiene.

4. **Stress management:** Prolonged stress can have negative effects on one's physical and emotional well-being. Engage in stress-reduction practices like yoga, progressive muscle relaxation, deep breathing, or mindfulness meditation. Take part in enjoyable and relaxing activities, including going on a nature walk, listening to music, or taking up a hobby.

5. **Social ties:** Having strong social ties is crucial for mental health. Try to keep up and cultivate your ties with friends, family, and neighbors. Participate in things like volunteering, attending social gatherings, or joining clubs that

promote a sense of community and belonging.

Useful Advice for Improving the Mind-Body Bond

- **Engage in mindfulness exercises:** Practice body scans or mindfulness meditation to develop awareness of your body and mind. Pay attention to your body: Be mindful of your bodily experiences and the connections they could have with your feelings or ideas.

- **Adopt holistic methods:** To encourage balance and relaxation, investigate complementary and alternative therapies including massage therapy, acupuncture, and aromatherapy.

- **Look for expert assistance:** Do not be afraid to seek help and assistance from a healthcare provider or mental health expert if you are experiencing problems with your physical or mental health.

Sources for Additional Research

- Centers for Disease Control and Prevention (CDC): Offers resources and information about how important exercise is for mental health.

- Research-based information about the relationship between mental and physical health is provided by the National Institute of Mental Health (NIMH).

- Bob Stahl & Elisha Goldstein's Mindfulness-Based Stress Reduction Workbook: a useful manual for applying mindfulness practices to reduce stress and improve general wellbeing.

- Local wellness centers or exercise classes: Look into ways to relieve stress and engage in physical activity in your neighborhood.

Through an awareness of the complex interrelationships between mental and physical health and deliberate lifestyle decisions, we may foster a stronger sense of resilience and well-being in our daily lives.

Chapter 3

Strategies for Stress Reduction

Although stress is an essential aspect of life, how we handle it can have a significant impact on both our physical and mental health. We will examine useful methods for recognizing and managing stress in this chapter, such as mindfulness, meditation, and relaxation exercises.

Recognizing Stress

Stress is the body's normal reaction to perceived dangers or difficulties. While occasional stress can be good for us, keeping us motivated and focused, prolonged or severe stress can negatively impact our health and wellbeing. Financial concerns, interpersonal problems, pressures from the workplace or school, and significant life transitions are common drivers of stress.

Techniques for Recognizing Stress

1. **Awareness**: Recognizing when you are under stress is the first step towards managing it. Keep an eye out for behavioral, emotional, and physical indicators of stress, such as tenseness in the muscles, agitation, trouble focusing, or irregularities in sleep patterns.

2. **Triggers**: Determine the precise circumstances, occurrences, or ideas that set off your stress reaction. You can spot reoccurring stressors and follow patterns by keeping a notebook.

3. **Customized Stressors:** Everybody has different stressors. Work

deadlines may cause stress for some people, but social settings or family disputes may cause it for others. Knowing what your personal triggers are will help you create focused coping mechanisms.

Techniques for relaxation, meditation, and mindfulness

Methods of Relaxation

Numerous methods of relaxation can aid in lowering stress levels and fostering serenity and relaxation.

- **Progressive muscle relaxation:** begin at your toes and work your way up to your head, tensing and relaxing various muscle groups in your body. This method can alleviate physical stress and encourage calmness.

- **Deep breathing exercises:** To trigger the body's relaxation response and lessen tension, practice deep breathing exercises like diaphragmatic breathing or box breathing.

- **Visualization:** Envision yourself in a tranquil setting, like a beach or forest, by using guided imagery or visualization techniques. As you vividly envision the sights, sounds, and sensations of your chosen location, use all of your senses.

Meditation

Training the mind to reach a state of concentrated awareness and attention is the goal of meditation. Frequent meditation practice can ease mental tension, promote general wellbeing, and quiet the mind.

- **Guided meditation:** To help you unwind and concentrate, use smartphone apps or guided meditation recordings. As a meditation instructor guides you through mindfulness exercises and relaxation techniques, follow along.

- **Loving-kindness meditation:** Practice loving-kindness meditation to develop compassion and kindness for both yourself and other people. Say affirmations like "May I be happy, may I be healthy, may I be safe" repeatedly while concentrating on fostering sentiments of kindness and compassion.

Mindfulness

Mindfulness is being open, curious, and accepting of the current moment while paying attention to it. By bringing awareness to your thoughts, feelings, and sensations without passing judgment, mindfulness exercises can help lower stress.

- **Mindful breathing:** Set aside some time each day to concentrate on your breathing while paying attention to how it feels to inhale and exhale. This easy exercise helps ease tension and promote mental calmness.

- **Body scan meditation:** Take a comfortable position, either lying down or sitting, and thoroughly scan your entire body, noting any points of tension or discomfort. Relaxation and stress relief can be achieved by paying attention to bodily sensations.

- **Mindful eating:** Take your time, enjoy every bite, and focus on the flavor, texture, and aroma of your food. Reducing stress-related eating and increasing meal enjoyment are two benefits of mindful eating.

- **Create a regular relaxing schedule:** Even if it's only for a short while, schedule time each day for activities that promote relaxation and reduce stress.

- **Make self-care a priority:** Give yourself the attention and resources you need by making time for hobbies, physical activity, and quality time with loved ones.

- **Establish boundaries**: Acquire the ability to decline obligations and pursuits that unnecessarily stress or overwhelm you.

- Seek assistance: In times of stress, seek advice and support from friends, family, or a mental health professional.

- **Headspace:** Provides mindfulness activities and guided meditation to help people relax and reduce stress.

- **Insight Timer:** Offers a variety of tools for meditation and relaxation, such as talks, music, and guided meditations.

- Matthew McKay, Martha Davis, and Elizabeth Robbins Eshelman's Relaxation and Stress Reduction Workbook: a thorough manual on stress reduction methods that includes breathing exercises, meditation, and mindfulness.

- Local yoga or meditation classes: Look into what your town has to offer in terms of in-person training and support.

You can create useful coping mechanisms for stress management and enhancing general well-being by implementing mindfulness, meditation, and relaxation practices into your everyday routine. Try out a variety of methods to see which one suits you the most, and keep in mind that in order to profit from these practices, consistency and repetition are essential.

Chapter 4

Building Resilience

Understanding resilience and its role in mental health

Resilience is the ability to bounce back from adversity, trauma, or other significant stressors and adapt to challenges in a healthy and constructive way. It is not about avoiding or denying difficult experiences but rather about facing them with courage, perseverance, and flexibility. Resilience plays a crucial role in mental health, helping individuals cope with life's ups and downs and thrive in the face of adversity.

Factors That Influence Resilience

1. **Social support:** Strong relationships with friends, family members, and community members provide a vital

source of support during challenging times. Having people you can turn to for emotional support, encouragement, and practical assistance can enhance resilience.

2. **Positive outlook:** Maintaining a hopeful and optimistic outlook can help individuals navigate difficult situations with greater resilience. Cultivating gratitude, focusing on strengths, and finding meaning and purpose in life can foster a positive mindset.

3. **Problem-solving skills:** Effective problem-solving skills enable individuals to identify solutions and take action to address challenges. Developing skills such as goal-setting, decision-making, and effective communication can enhance resilience.

4. **Coping strategies:** Healthy coping strategies, such as seeking social support, practicing self-care, and engaging in relaxation techniques, can help individuals manage stress and build resilience. Avoiding harmful coping mechanisms, such as substance abuse or avoidance behaviors, is also important.

Practical Ways to Cultivate Resilience in Everyday Life

1. **Develop self-awareness:** Take time to reflect on your strengths, weaknesses, and coping strategies. Understanding your own resilience can help you navigate challenges more effectively.

2. **Cultivate optimism:** Focus on the positive aspects of situations, even in the face of adversity. Practice

reframing negative thoughts and finding silver linings in difficult experiences.

3. **Build strong relationships:** invest time and effort into nurturing relationships with friends, family members, and supportive individuals in your community. Reach out for help and support when you need it, and offer support to others in return.

4. **Practice self-care:** Prioritize your physical, emotional, and mental well-being by engaging in activities that promote relaxation, stress reduction, and overall health. This may include exercise, mindfulness, hobbies, or spending time in nature.

5. **Set realistic goals:** Break larger goals into smaller, manageable steps, and celebrate your progress along the

way. Setting and achieving goals can boost confidence and resilience.

6. **Foster adaptability:** embrace change and uncertainty as opportunities for growth and learning. Cultivate flexibility and resilience by developing a mindset that is open to new experiences and challenges.

7. **Seek meaning and purpose:** Identify what matters most to you and find ways to incorporate meaning and purpose into your daily life. Connecting with your values and passions can provide a sense of direction and resilience during difficult times.

8. **Learn from setbacks:** View setbacks and failures as opportunities for learning and growth rather than as reflections of your worth or abilities. Reflect on what you can learn from

difficult experiences and how you can use that knowledge to navigate future challenges.

9. **Practice gratitude:** Take time each day to reflect on the things you are grateful for, no matter how small. Cultivating an attitude of gratitude can foster resilience and enhance overall well-being.

10. **Seek support when needed:** Don't hesitate to reach out for help and support from friends, family members, or mental health professionals when facing significant challenges or experiencing emotional distress. Asking for help is a sign of strength, not weakness.

Resources for Further Exploration

- The Resilience Factor by Karen Reivich and Andrew Shatte offers practical strategies for building resilience and coping with adversity.

- **Resilience:** The Science of Mastering Life's Greatest Challenges by Steven M. Southwick and Dennis S. Charney: Explores the science of resilience and provides insights into how individuals can cultivate resilience in their lives.

- **Local support groups or therapy:** Explore opportunities for connecting with others who have experienced similar challenges and can provide support and encouragement.

By cultivating resilience in everyday life, individuals can develop the strength and flexibility needed to navigate life's challenges with grace and confidence. Remember that resilience is a skill that can be developed and

strengthened over time with practice and
perseverance.

Chapter 5

Navigating Emotions

Emotions are an integral part of the human experience, influencing how we perceive and interact with the world around us. While emotions can be both pleasurable and challenging, learning to navigate them effectively is essential for maintaining mental health and well-being. In this chapter, we will explore emotion regulation skills for managing intense feelings and coping mechanisms for dealing with anger, sadness, and anxiety.

Understanding Emotion Regulation

Emotion regulation refers to the ability to recognize, understand, and manage one's emotions in healthy and adaptive ways. Effective emotion regulation allows individuals to respond to situations with clarity, resilience, and flexibility, rather than reacting impulsively or becoming overwhelmed by intense emotions. Developing emotion regulation skills is crucial for maintaining emotional balance and mental well-being.

Managing intense feelings

1. **Recognize and acknowledge emotions:** The first step in emotion regulation is to become aware of and acknowledge your feelings. Pay attention to physical sensations, thoughts, and behaviors that accompany different emotions.

2. Identify triggers: identify the specific situations, events, or thoughts that trigger intense emotions. Understanding your triggers can help you anticipate and prepare for emotional reactions.

3. **Practice mindfulness:** Mindfulness techniques, such as mindfulness meditation or deep breathing exercises, can help you stay grounded and present in the moment, allowing you to observe and accept your emotions without judgment.

4. **Challenge negative thoughts:** Negative thoughts and beliefs can fuel intense emotions such as anger, sadness, or anxiety. Practice cognitive restructuring techniques to challenge and reframe negative thinking patterns.

Coping mechanisms for anger

1. Take a time-out. If you feel yourself becoming angry or agitated, take a break from the situation to cool down. Walk away, take deep breaths, or

engage in a calming activity until you feel calmer and more composed.

2. Express emotions constructively. Find healthy ways to express and communicate your anger, such as talking to a trusted friend or writing in a journal. Avoid lashing out or engaging in aggressive behavior.

3. Practice relaxation techniques: Engage in relaxation techniques, such as progressive muscle relaxation or deep breathing exercises, to reduce physical tension and promote a sense of calm.

Coping mechanisms for sadness

1. **Allow yourself to feel:** It's important to allow yourself to experience sadness and acknowledge your feelings without judgment. Suppressing or denying emotions can

prolong feelings of sadness and make them more difficult to manage.

2. **Engage in self-care activities**: Take care of yourself by engaging in activities that bring you comfort and joy, such as spending time with loved ones, engaging in hobbies, or practicing relaxation techniques.

3. **Seek support:** Reach out to friends, family members, or a mental health professional for support and comfort during times of sadness. Talking to someone you trust can help you feel less alone and more supported.

Coping mechanisms for anxiety

1. **Practice relaxation techniques:** Practice relaxation techniques, such as deep breathing exercises, progressive muscle relaxation, or guided imagery, to calm your mind

and body and reduce feelings of anxiety.

2. **Challenge anxious thoughts:** Identify and challenge irrational or exaggerated thoughts that contribute to feelings of anxiety. Replace negative thoughts with more realistic and balanced perspectives.

3. **Engage in activities that promote relaxation:** Engage in activities that promote relaxation and stress relief, such as exercise, yoga, or spending time in nature. Find activities that bring you joy and help distract your mind from anxious thoughts.

Practical Tips for Navigating Emotions

- **Practice self-compassion:** Be kind and compassionate toward yourself, especially during difficult emotional experiences. Treat yourself with the same kindness and understanding that you would offer a friend.

- **Develop a toolbox of coping strategies:** Experiment with different coping mechanisms and strategies for managing intense emotions. Find what works best for you, and incorporate these techniques into your daily routine.

- **Seek professional help when needed**: If you're struggling to manage intense emotions or experiencing significant distress, don't hesitate to seek support from a mental health professional. Therapy can provide you with the tools and support you need to navigate difficult emotions and improve your emotional well-being.

- The Dialectical Behavior Therapy Skills Workbook by Matthew McKay, Jeffrey C. Wood, and Jeffrey Brantley offers practical exercises and techniques for managing intense emotions using dialectical behavior therapy (DBT) skills.

- MindShift is a free app developed by Anxiety Canada that provides tools and resources for managing anxiety and coping with intense emotions.

- **Local support groups or therapy:** explore opportunities for connecting with others who are experiencing similar challenges and can provide support and encouragement.

By developing emotion regulation skills and implementing effective coping mechanisms, you can navigate intense feelings with greater ease and resilience. Remember that managing emotions is a skill that can be learned and strengthened over time with practice and patience.

Chapter 6

The Power of Self-Compassion

Self-compassion is the practice of treating oneself with kindness, understanding, and acceptance, especially in times of difficulty or failure. It involves extending the same compassion and empathy to ourselves that we would offer to a close friend or loved one. In this chapter, we will explore the importance of self-compassion in mental health and provide practical strategies for cultivating self-compassion and self-love.

Importance of Self-Compassion in Mental Health

Self-compassion plays a crucial role in promoting mental health and well-being. Research has shown that individuals who practice self-compassion are more resilient in the face of challenges, have lower levels of anxiety and depression, and experience greater overall life satisfaction. Here are some ways in which self-compassion can benefit mental health:

1. **Reducing self-criticism:** Self-compassion involves replacing self-criticism and harsh judgment with kindness and understanding. By treating ourselves with compassion, we can break free from the cycle of negative self-talk and cultivate a more positive and supportive inner dialogue.

2. **Building resilience:** Self-compassion allows us to acknowledge and validate our own emotions and experiences, even when they are difficult or painful. By practicing self-compassion, we develop greater emotional resilience

and are better able to navigate life's challenges with grace and strength.

3. **Enhancing emotional well-being:** Self-compassion fosters a greater sense of emotional well-being by promoting self-acceptance and self-love. When we treat ourselves with kindness and compassion, we experience greater feelings of contentment, peace, and happiness.

Practices for Developing Self-Compassion and Self-Love

1. **Cultivate mindfulness:** Mindfulness involves bringing awareness to the present moment with openness, curiosity, and acceptance. Practice mindfulness exercises to observe your thoughts and feelings without judgment, allowing yourself to

experience whatever arises with kindness and compassion.

2. **Practice self-kindness:** Treat yourself with the same kindness and understanding that you would offer to a close friend or loved one. When faced with difficult emotions or challenges, respond with words of encouragement and support rather than criticism or judgment.

3. **Challenge self-critical thoughts:** Notice when you engage in self-critical or negative self-talk and challenge these thoughts with compassion and understanding. Ask yourself, "Would I speak to a friend in this way?" and reframe your thoughts with kindness and self-compassion.

4. **Cultivate gratitude:** Practice gratitude by focusing on the things in

your life that you are thankful for, no matter how small. Gratitude can help shift your perspective from one of lack or self-criticism to one of abundance and appreciation.

5. **Set boundaries:** Prioritize your own needs and well-being by setting boundaries with others and saying no to commitments or activities that drain your energy or detract from your self-care. Remember that self-compassion also means honoring your own limitations and taking care of yourself.

6. **Practice self-care:** Make self-care a priority by engaging in activities that nourish your mind, body, and soul. This may include exercise, meditation, spending time in nature, or engaging in hobbies or creative

pursuits that bring you joy and fulfillment.

7. **Seek support:** Reach out to friends, family members, or a therapist for support and encouragement when you need it. Remember that it's okay to ask for help and that seeking support is a sign of strength, not weakness.

Practical Tips for Cultivating Self-Compassion

- Start small: Begin by practicing self-compassion in small, everyday moments. Notice when you're being self-critical and respond with kindness and understanding.

- Practice self-compassion exercises: Try journaling, meditation, or guided imagery exercises specifically designed to cultivate self-compassion and self-love.

- Be patient and gentle with yourself. Developing self-compassion is a process that takes time and practice. Be patient with yourself, and remember that it's okay to have setbacks along the way.

Resources for Further Exploration

- **Self-Compassion:** The Proven Power of Being Kind to Yourself by Kristin Neff: Offers practical exercises and techniques for cultivating self-compassion and overcoming self-criticism.

- **The Mindful Self-Compassion** Workbook by Kristin Neff and Christopher Germer provides step-by-step guidance for developing mindfulness and self-compassion skills through exercises, meditations, and reflections.

- **Local support groups or therapy**: Explore opportunities for connecting with others who are working on cultivating self-compassion and self-love in their own lives.

By practicing self-compassion and self-love, we can cultivate a greater sense of well-being, resilience, and inner peace. Remember that self-compassion is a skill that can be developed and strengthened over time with practice and patience. Treat yourself with kindness and compassion, and remember that you are worthy of love and acceptance just as you are.

Chapter 7

Cultivating Positive Relationships

Positive and meaningful relationships play a vital role in our mental well-being, providing support, connection, and a sense of belonging. In this chapter, we will explore the impact of social connections on mental health and provide strategies for fostering healthy relationships and setting boundaries.

Impact of Social Connections on Mental Well-Being

Research has consistently shown that social connections are closely linked to mental health and well-being. Strong and supportive relationships can provide a buffer against stress, reduce feelings of loneliness and isolation, and contribute to greater overall happiness and life satisfaction. Here are some ways in which social connections impact mental well-being:

1. **Emotional support:** Close relationships with friends, family members, and loved ones provide a source of emotional support during times of stress, sadness, or difficulty. Having someone to talk to and lean on can help alleviate feelings of loneliness and provide comfort and reassurance.

2. **Sense of belonging:** Social connections give us a sense of belonging and connection to others, which is essential for our mental and emotional health. Feeling connected to a community or social group can provide a sense of purpose and identity, as well as opportunities for growth and personal development.

3. **Increased resilience:** Strong social connections can enhance resilience and help us cope with life's challenges more effectively. Knowing that we have a support network of friends and family members who care about us can give us the strength and courage to face adversity with greater resilience and confidence.

Strategies for Fostering Healthy Relationships

1. **Prioritize communication:**
   Effective communication is key to building and maintaining healthy relationships. Practice active listening, empathy, and open communication with your loved ones, and be willing to express your needs and feelings honestly and assertively.

2. **Nurture trust and intimacy:** Build trust and intimacy in your relationships by being reliable, honest, and supportive. Foster a sense of closeness and connection by sharing your thoughts, feelings, and experiences with your loved ones.

3. **Show appreciation and gratitude:** Express appreciation and gratitude for the people in your life by acknowledging their contributions, expressing gratitude for their support, and showing them that you care. Small gestures of kindness and appreciation can go a long way in strengthening relationships.

4. **Spend quality time together:** Make time for meaningful interactions and shared activities with your loved ones. Whether it's having a meal together, going for a walk, or

engaging in a hobby or shared interest, spending quality time together strengthens bonds and fosters connection.

Setting boundaries in relationships

1. **Know your limits:** Take time to identify your own needs, preferences, and boundaries in relationships. Be clear about what is acceptable and unacceptable behavior for you, and communicate your boundaries assertively and respectfully.

2. **Practice assertiveness:** assertive communication involves expressing your needs, thoughts, and feelings in a clear and respectful manner while also respecting the needs and boundaries of others. Practice assertive communication skills to set

boundaries and advocate for yourself effectively.

3. **Say no when necessary:** Don't be afraid to say no to requests, demands, or invitations that don't align with your values, priorities, or boundaries. Saying no is an important part of setting healthy boundaries and taking care of yourself.

4. **Respect others' boundaries:** Just as you have boundaries, it's important to respect the boundaries of others. Pay attention to cues and signals from your loved ones indicating their comfort level and boundaries, and respect their need for space and autonomy.

- **Be present:** Make an effort to be fully present and engaged in your interactions with others. Put away distractions, such as phones or electronic devices, and give your full attention to the person you're with.

- **Practice empathy and compassion:** Put yourself in the shoes of others and try to understand their thoughts, feelings, and perspectives. Show empathy and compassion by offering support, validation, and understanding.

- **Seek support when needed:** Don't hesitate to reach out to friends, family members, or a therapist for support and guidance in navigating relationships and setting boundaries.

Seeking support is a sign of strength, not weakness.

- **Boundaries:** Where You End and I Begin by Anne Katherine: Offers practical guidance and exercises for setting healthy boundaries in relationships and taking care of yourself.
- The Gottman Institute provides resources and workshops on building and maintaining healthy relationships, including communication skills, conflict resolution, and fostering intimacy.
- **Therapy or counseling:** Consider seeking support from a licensed therapist or counselor if you're struggling with relationship issues or finding it challenging to set

boundaries. A therapist can provide you with personalized guidance and support in navigating relationships and improving your mental well-being.

By prioritizing communication, nurturing trust and intimacy, and setting healthy boundaries, you can cultivate positive and meaningful relationships that contribute to greater mental well-being and overall happiness. Remember that building and maintaining healthy relationships is an ongoing process that requires effort, patience, and commitment from all parties involved.

Chapter 8

Sleep Hygiene and Mental Health

Sleep is not just a luxury; it's a fundamental pillar of mental wellness. In this chapter, we'll explore the crucial link between sleep and mental health and provide practical tips for improving sleep quality and establishing a bedtime routine.

The Link Between Sleep and Mental Wellness

Quality sleep is essential for maintaining optimal mental health and well-being. Sleep plays a critical role in various cognitive functions, emotional regulation, and stress management. When we don't get enough sleep or experience poor sleep quality, it can have profound effects on our mental wellness, including:

1. **Mood regulation:** Sleep deprivation can disrupt mood-regulating neurotransmitters in the brain, leading to increased irritability, mood swings, and symptoms of depression and anxiety.

2. **Cognitive function:** Adequate sleep is necessary for optimal cognitive function, including attention, memory, and problem-solving skills. Poor sleep can impair cognitive performance, leading to difficulties in concentration, decision-making, and productivity.

3. **Stress management:** Sleep deprivation can increase levels of stress hormones like cortisol, leading to heightened stress responses and difficulty coping with daily stressors.

4. **Emotional regulation:** Quality sleep is essential for regulating emotions

and processing emotional experiences. Lack of sleep can lead to heightened emotional reactivity, impulsivity, and difficulty managing negative emotions.

Tips for Improving Sleep Quality and Establishing a Bedtime Routine

1. **Maintain a consistent sleep schedule:** go to bed and wake up at the same time every day, even on weekends. Consistency helps regulate your body's internal clock and improves overall sleep quality.

2. **Create a relaxing bedtime routine:** Establish a calming bedtime routine to signal to your body that it's time to wind down. This may include activities such as reading, taking a warm bath, practicing relaxation techniques like deep breathing or

meditation, or listening to soothing music.

3. **Create a comfortable sleep environment:** Make sure your bedroom is conducive to sleep by keeping it cool, dark, and quiet. Invest in a comfortable mattress and pillows, and remove electronic devices that emit blue light, which can disrupt sleep.

4. **Limit exposure to screens before bed:** Avoid using electronic devices such as smartphones, tablets, and computers before bedtime, as the blue light emitted by these devices can interfere with your body's natural sleep-wake cycle.

5. **Avoid stimulants and heavy meals before bed:** Avoid consuming caffeine, nicotine, and heavy meals close to bedtime, as these can

interfere with your ability to fall asleep and stay asleep.

6. **Get regular exercise:** Engage in regular physical activity during the day, but avoid vigorous exercise close to bedtime, as it can be stimulating and make it harder to fall asleep.

7. **Manage stress and anxiety:** Practice stress-reduction techniques such as mindfulness meditation, deep breathing exercises, or progressive muscle relaxation to help calm your mind and promote relaxation before bedtime.

8. **Limit naps:** While short naps can be beneficial for some people, avoid taking long or late afternoon naps, as they can disrupt your sleep-wake cycle and make it harder to fall asleep at night.

- **Keep a sleep diary:** Keep track of your sleep habits, including bedtime, wake time, and any factors that may affect your sleep quality, such as caffeine intake, exercise, or stress levels.

- **Gradually adjust your sleep schedule:** If you need to change your sleep schedule, such as adjusting to a new work schedule or traveling to a different time zone, gradually shift your bedtime and wake time by 15–30 minutes each day until you reach your desired schedule.

- **Consider seeking professional help:** If you continue to experience difficulties with sleep despite implementing good sleep hygiene practices, consider seeking help from a healthcare professional, such as a sleep specialist or therapist, who can provide further evaluation and treatment options.

Resources for Further Exploration

- The National Sleep Foundation offers resources and information on sleep health, including tips for improving sleep quality and establishing a bedtime routine.

- **Sleep Cycle:** A smartphone app that tracks your sleep patterns and provides insights into your sleep quality, helping you identify factors that may be affecting your sleep.

- Cognitive Behavioral Therapy for Insomnia (CBT-I): CBT-I is a highly effective treatment for insomnia that addresses the underlying thoughts and behaviors that contribute to sleep difficulties. Consider seeking therapy from a licensed therapist trained in CBT-I if you're struggling with chronic insomnia.

By prioritizing sleep hygiene and establishing a consistent bedtime routine, you can improve your sleep quality and enhance your overall mental wellness. Remember that quality sleep is an essential component of a healthy lifestyle and plays a crucial role in supporting your mental health and well-being.

Chapter 9

Nutrition and Mental Health

Nutrition plays a significant role in maintaining good mental health by influencing brain function, mood regulation, and overall well-being. In this chapter, we will explore the role of diet in mental health and discuss foods that support brain function and mood regulation.

The Role of Diet in Maintaining Good Mental Health

The food we eat provides the nutrients necessary for optimal brain function and mental health. Research has shown that certain dietary patterns and nutrients can influence mood, cognition, and mental well-being. Here are some ways in which diet can impact mental health:

1. **Brain function:** The brain requires a steady supply of nutrients to function properly, including vitamins, minerals, antioxidants, and omega-3 fatty acids. A balanced and nutritious diet can support cognitive function, memory, and concentration.

2. **Mood regulation:** Certain foods and nutrients can influence neurotransmitter production and activity in the brain, affecting mood regulation and emotional well-being. Nutrient deficiencies or imbalances can contribute to mood disorders such as depression and anxiety.

3. **Inflammation:** Chronic inflammation has been linked to the development of mental health conditions such as depression and schizophrenia. Consuming an anti-inflammatory diet rich in fruits,

vegetables, whole grains, and healthy fats can help reduce inflammation and support mental health.

Foods That Support Brain Function and Mood Regulation

1. **Fatty fish:** Fatty fish such as salmon, mackerel, and sardines are rich in omega-3 fatty acids, which are essential for brain health and mood regulation. Omega-3 fatty acids have been shown to reduce inflammation, improve mood, and support cognitive function.

2. **Leafy greens:** Leafy green vegetables such as spinach, kale, and Swiss chard are packed with vitamins, minerals, and antioxidants that support brain health. They are particularly rich in folate, which has

been linked to a reduced risk of depression.

3. **Berries:** Berries such as blueberries, strawberries, and blackberries are rich in antioxidants, which help protect the brain from oxidative stress and inflammation. Studies have shown that regular consumption of berries may improve cognitive function and delay age-related decline in brain function.

4. **Nuts and seeds:** Nuts and seeds are excellent sources of healthy fats, vitamins, minerals, and antioxidants that support brain health. Walnuts, almonds, flaxseeds, and chia seeds are particularly rich in omega-3 fatty acids and other nutrients beneficial for mental health.

5. **Whole grains:** Whole grains such as oats, quinoa, brown rice, and barley

provide a steady source of energy for the brain and support stable blood sugar levels. Consuming whole grains can help improve mood, concentration, and cognitive function.

6. **Fermented foods:** Fermented foods such as yogurt, kefir, sauerkraut, and kimchi contain beneficial probiotics that support gut health and may have a positive impact on mood and mental health. The gut-brain connection suggests that a healthy gut microbiome is essential for optimal brain function and emotional well-being.

7. **Dark chocolate:** Dark chocolate contains flavonoids and antioxidants that have been shown to improve mood, reduce stress, and enhance cognitive function. Choose dark

chocolate with a high cocoa content (70% or higher) for maximum benefits.

Practical Tips for Incorporating Brain-Boosting Foods into Your Diet

- Start your day with a balanced breakfast that includes foods rich in protein, healthy fats, and complex carbohydrates to fuel your brain and stabilize your mood.
- Incorporate a variety of colorful fruits and vegetables into your meals and snacks to ensure you're getting a wide range of vitamins, minerals, and antioxidants.
- Include sources of omega-3 fatty acids in your diet at least twice a week, such as fatty fish, flaxseeds, walnuts, or chia seeds.

- Experiment with new recipes and cooking methods to make healthy eating enjoyable and sustainable.
- Be mindful of portion sizes and aim for a balanced diet that includes a variety of nutrient-dense foods from all food groups.

Resources for Further Exploration

- The Brain Health Food Guide by Dr. Leslie Korn provides practical guidance and recipes for incorporating brain-boosting foods into your diet to support mental health and cognitive function.
- The Mindful Diet by Ruth Wolever and Beth Reardon offers strategies for cultivating mindfulness and making healthy eating choices that support mental and emotional well-being.

- Local farmer markets or community-supported agriculture (CSA) programs: Explore opportunities to purchase fresh, locally grown produce and support sustainable agriculture practices in your community.

By prioritizing balanced and nutritious diet rich in brain-boosting foods, you can support your mental health and well-being and enhance cognitive function, mood regulation, and overall vitality. Remember that small changes to your diet can have a significant impact on your mental health and that eating well is an essential component of a holistic approach to mental wellness.

Chapter 10

Exercise for the Mind

Physical activity is not just beneficial for your body; it also has powerful effects on your mental well-being. In this chapter, we'll explore the benefits of exercise for mental health and provide practical tips for incorporating physical activity into your daily life for optimal mental wellness.

Benefits of Physical Activity for Mental Well-Being

Regular exercise has numerous positive effects on mental health, including:

1. **Stress reduction:** Exercise helps reduce levels of stress hormones such as cortisol and adrenaline, leading to a calmer and more relaxed state of mind.

2. **Mood enhancement:** Physical activity stimulates the release of endorphins, neurotransmitters that boost mood and promote feelings of happiness and well-being.

3. **Anxiety relief:** Exercise has been shown to reduce symptoms of anxiety and panic disorders by providing a distraction from worrisome thoughts and promoting relaxation.

4. **Improved sleep:** Regular exercise can improve sleep quality and duration, leading to better rest and enhanced mental clarity and concentration.

5. **Enhanced cognitive function:** Physical activity has been linked to improved cognitive function, including better memory, attention, and decision-making skills.

6. **Increased self-esteem:** Regular exercise can boost self-esteem and self-confidence by promoting feelings of accomplishment and empowerment.

Incorporating Exercise into Daily Life for Optimal Mental Health

1. **Find activities you enjoy:** Choose physical activities that you enjoy and look forward to, whether it's walking, jogging, cycling, dancing, swimming, or playing sports. Finding activities that you find enjoyable makes it more likely that you'll stick with them long-term.

2. **Start small and set realistic goals:** Begin with manageable amounts of exercise and gradually increase intensity and duration as your fitness level improves. Set achievable goals

that are specific, measurable, and realistic, and celebrate your progress along the way.

3. **Make it a habit.** Schedule regular exercise sessions into your daily or weekly routine, just like you would any other important appointment. Consistency is key to reaping the mental health benefits of exercise.

4. **Be flexible:** Be flexible and creative in finding opportunities to be physically active throughout your day, even if you have a busy schedule. Take the stairs instead of the elevator, walk or bike to work if possible, or incorporate short bursts of activity into your breaks.

5. **Mix it up:** Keep your exercise routine interesting and engaging by varying your activities and trying new things. Incorporate a mix of aerobic, strength

training, and flexibility exercises to reap the full range of physical and mental health benefits.

6. **Find social support:** Exercise with friends, family members, or join a group fitness class or sports team to make physical activity more enjoyable and motivating. Social support can help you stay accountable and committed to your exercise goals.

7. **Listen to your body:** Pay attention to how your body feels during and after exercise, and adjust your intensity and duration accordingly. It's important to challenge yourself but also to rest and recover when needed to prevent injury and burnout.

- **Take advantage of technology:** Use fitness apps, wearable activity trackers, or online workout videos to find inspiration, track your progress, and stay motivated.

- **Make it fun:** Choose activities that you genuinely enjoy and look forward to, whether it's dancing to your favorite music, playing a sport with friends, or exploring nature through hiking or outdoor activities.

- **Be mindful:** Practice mindfulness while exercising by paying attention to your body and the sensations you experience during physical activity. Focus on your breathing, posture, and movement, and let go of distractions and worries.

- The Exercise Cure by Jordan Metzl explores the science behind the mental health benefits of exercise and provides practical strategies for incorporating physical activity into your life.

- Local gyms, community centers, or parks and recreation departments: Explore opportunities for group fitness classes, sports leagues, or recreational activities in your area.

- **Therapy or counseling:** Consider seeking support from a therapist or counselor who can help you overcome barriers to exercise and develop a personalized plan for incorporating physical activity into your mental wellness routine.

By making physical activity a regular part of your daily life, you can harness its powerful benefits for mental health and well-being. Remember that exercise doesn't have to be strenuous or time-consuming to be effective; even small amounts of activity can make a big difference in how you feel both physically and mentally.

Chapter 11

Seeking Help: Therapy and Counseling

Seeking professional help through therapy and counseling is a courageous and important step toward improving mental health and well-being. In this chapter, we'll explore the different types of therapy, overcome stigma, and address barriers to seeking professional help.

Understanding the Different Types of Therapy

Therapy, also known as counseling or psychotherapy, encompasses a wide range of approaches and techniques designed to help individuals address emotional, psychological, and behavioral challenges. **Here are some common types of therapy:**

1. **Cognitive Behavioral Therapy (CBT):** CBT is a widely used and evidence-based therapy that focuses on identifying and challenging negative thought patterns and behaviors. It aims to help individuals develop more adaptive ways of thinking and coping with difficult emotions and situations.

2. **Psychodynamic Therapy:** Psychodynamic therapy explores unconscious thoughts and emotions, often rooted in childhood experiences and relationships. It emphasizes self-reflection, insight, and understanding of how past experiences influence present behavior and relationships.

3. **Humanistic Therapy:** Humanistic therapy emphasizes self-exploration, personal growth, and self-actualization. It encourages

individuals to tap into their inner resources, strengths, and values to find solutions to their problems and live more fulfilling lives.

4. **Acceptance and Commitment Therapy (ACT):** ACT focuses on accepting uncomfortable thoughts and feelings rather than trying to change or control them. It emphasizes mindfulness, acceptance, and commitment to taking meaningful action aligned with one's values.

5. **Dialectical Behavior Therapy (DBT):** DBT combines elements of CBT with mindfulness-based techniques to help individuals regulate emotions, improve interpersonal relationships, and cope with distressing situations. It's particularly effective for individuals

with borderline personality disorder and emotion dysregulation.

6. **Family Therapy:** Family therapy involves working with couples or families to address relational issues, improve communication, and resolve conflicts. It recognizes the interconnectedness of family dynamics and aims to promote understanding and cooperation among family members.

Overcoming Stigma and Barriers to Seeking Professional Help

Despite the proven effectiveness of therapy, stigma and misconceptions surrounding mental health treatment can prevent individuals from seeking help. Here are some strategies for overcoming stigma and barriers to seeking professional help:

1. **Educate yourself:** Learn about mental health conditions, treatment options, and the benefits of therapy. Understanding that mental health struggles are common and treatable can help reduce stigma and increase the willingness to seek help.

2. **Challenge negative beliefs:** Challenge negative beliefs and attitudes about therapy and mental health treatment. Recognize that seeking help is a sign of strength and courage, not weakness or failure.

3. **Talk openly about mental health:** Break the silence surrounding mental health by talking openly and honestly about your own experiences or by supporting others who may be struggling. By sharing your story, you can help reduce stigma and create a

supportive environment for seeking help.

4. **Seek support from trusted individuals:** Reach out to friends, family members, or other trusted individuals for support and encouragement. Having a supportive network can provide reassurance and validation and help overcome fears or doubts about seeking help.

5. **Consider online therapy options:** If traditional therapy settings feel intimidating or inaccessible, consider exploring online therapy platforms that offer convenient and flexible options for receiving support from licensed therapists or counselors.

6. **Start with small steps:** Begin by exploring therapy options and scheduling an initial consultation with a therapist or counselor. Taking

small steps toward seeking help can help build confidence and reduce anxiety about the process.

Practical Tips for Finding a Therapist or Counselor

- **Research therapy options:** Take the time to research different therapy approaches and therapists or counselors who specialize in areas relevant to your needs and preferences.

- **Ask for recommendations:** Seek recommendations from trusted individuals, such as friends, family members, or healthcare providers, who have experience with therapy or counseling.

- **Interview potential therapists:** Schedule initial consultations with potential therapists or counselors to discuss your concerns, goals, and treatment approach. Trust your instincts and choose someone with whom you feel comfortable and supported.

- **Consider affordability and accessibility:** Explore therapy options that are affordable and accessible to you, whether through insurance coverage, sliding scale fees, or community mental health resources.

Resources for Further Exploration

- Psychology Today offers a searchable directory of therapists and counselors, as well as articles and resources on mental health and therapy.
- The National Alliance on Mental Illness (NAMI) provides information, support, and advocacy for individuals

and families affected by mental health conditions, including resources on finding mental health treatment.

- **Online therapy platforms:** Explore online therapy platforms such as BetterHelp, Talkspace, or BetterUp that offer convenient and accessible options for receiving therapy or counseling from licensed professionals.

Remember that seeking help is a brave and proactive step toward improving your mental health and well-being. Whether you're struggling with specific challenges or seeking personal growth and self-discovery, therapy and counseling can provide valuable support, insight, and guidance on your journey toward healing and self-empowerment.

Chapter 12

Medication and Mental Health

Medication can be an essential component of treatment for many mental health conditions, offering relief from symptoms and improving overall quality of life. In this chapter, we'll explore the role of medication in treating mental illnesses, along with the risks, benefits, and considerations for medication management.

Exploring the Role of Medication in Treating Mental Illnesses

Medication plays a crucial role in the treatment of various mental health conditions, including depression, anxiety disorders, bipolar disorder, schizophrenia, and others. While therapy, lifestyle changes, and support are often integral parts of treatment, medication can help address chemical imbalances in the brain and alleviate symptoms that may be difficult to manage through other means.

Here are some key points to consider about the role of medication in treating mental illnesses:

1. **Target symptoms:** Medications are often prescribed to target specific symptoms associated with mental health conditions, such as low mood, anxiety, hallucinations, or mood swings. Different medications may be used to address different symptoms or aspects of a condition.

2. **Chemical imbalance:** Many mental health conditions are believed to involve imbalances in neurotransmitters, the brain's chemical messengers. Medications work by altering the levels or activity

of these neurotransmitters to restore balance and alleviate symptoms.

3. **Individualized treatment:** Treatment with medication is highly individualized, and the type of medication prescribed will depend on factors such as the specific diagnosis, severity of symptoms, medical history, and individual response to treatment.

4. **Combination therapy:** In some cases, a combination of medication and therapy may be the most effective approach to treatment. Therapy can help individuals learn coping skills, address underlying issues, and make behavioral changes, while medication can provide relief from symptoms and support therapy outcomes.

While medication can be highly effective in treating mental health conditions, it's important to weigh the risks and benefits and consider various factors when managing medication. Here are some considerations to keep in mind:

1. **Potential side effects:** Like any medication, psychiatric medications can cause side effects, ranging from mild to severe. Common side effects may include drowsiness, weight gain, sexual dysfunction, gastrointestinal upset, or changes in appetite. It's essential to discuss potential side effects with your healthcare provider and report any concerns promptly.

2. **Monitoring and adjustment**: Medication management often involves ongoing monitoring and

adjustment to ensure optimal effectiveness and minimize side effects. Your healthcare provider may periodically review your symptoms, adjust dosages, or switch medications if necessary.

3. **Compliance and adherence:** Consistency and adherence to medication regimens are crucial for achieving positive outcomes. It's essential to take medications as prescribed, follow dosage instructions carefully, and communicate openly with your healthcare provider about any challenges or concerns you may have.

4. **Withdrawal and discontinuation:** Some medications may cause withdrawal symptoms or require a gradual tapering off to discontinue safely. It's important to work closely

with your healthcare provider to develop a plan for discontinuing medication if needed and to avoid stopping abruptly without medical guidance.

5. **Stigma and misconceptions:** There can be stigma and misconceptions surrounding psychiatric medication, which may deter some individuals from seeking treatment or adhering to prescribed regimens. It's important to challenge stigma, educate yourself about the benefits and risks of medication, and make informed decisions based on your individual needs and circumstances.

Practical Tips for Medication Management

- **Keep a medication journal:** Maintain a record of your

medications, including dosages, frequency, and any side effects or changes in symptoms you experience. This can help you track your progress and communicate effectively with your healthcare provider.

- **Establish a routine:** Take your medications at the same time each day and incorporate them into your daily routine to help ensure consistency and adherence.

- **Communicate openly:** Keep open lines of communication with your healthcare provider and discuss any questions, concerns, or changes in symptoms you experience. Your healthcare provider can provide guidance and support throughout your treatment journey.

- **Seek support:** Connect with support groups, online forums, or peer support networks for individuals living with mental health conditions and share experiences, insights, and strategies for medication management.

Resources for Further Exploration

- The National Institute of Mental Health (NIMH) provides information and resources on mental health conditions, treatment options, and medication management.

- Mental Health America (MHA) offers educational materials, advocacy, and support for individuals living with mental health conditions, including resources on medication and treatment.

- RxList provides comprehensive information on prescription medications, including side effects, drug interactions, and dosage guidelines.

Remember that medication is just one tool in the toolbox for managing mental health conditions, and treatment decisions should be made in collaboration with your healthcare provider based on your individual needs and preferences. By staying informed, communicating openly, and actively participating in your treatment plan, you can optimize the benefits of medication and enhance your overall mental health and well-being.

Chapter 13

Finding Balance in Work and Life

In today's fast-paced world, finding balance between work and life can be challenging yet essential for maintaining mental well-being and overall satisfaction. In this chapter, we'll explore strategies for managing work-related stress and achieving a healthy work-life balance, emphasizing the importance of setting boundaries and prioritizing self-care.

Strategies for Managing Work-Related Stress

1. **Prioritize tasks**: identify the most important tasks and deadlines, and focus your energy on completing them first. Break larger projects into smaller, manageable tasks to avoid feeling overwhelmed.

2. **Delegate when possible:** Learn to delegate tasks to colleagues or team members when appropriate. Delegating not only helps lighten your workload but also fosters collaboration and teamwork.

3. **Practice time management:** Use tools such as calendars, planners, or task management apps to organize your schedule and prioritize your time effectively. Set aside dedicated time for work, breaks, and leisure activities to maintain a healthy balance.

4. **Set realistic expectations:** Be realistic about what you can accomplish within a given timeframe and communicate openly with your supervisor or colleagues about workload and deadlines. Setting realistic expectations can help reduce stress and prevent burnout.

5. **Take regular breaks:** Incorporate short breaks into your workday to rest and recharge. Use breaks to stretch, go for a walk, or engage in activities that help clear your mind and reduce stress.

6. **Practice mindfulness:** Incorporate mindfulness practices into your daily routine to help manage stress and promote a sense of calm and relaxation. Mindfulness techniques such as deep breathing, meditation, or mindful eating can help you stay present and focused amid the demands of work.

Achieving work-life balance

1. **Set boundaries**: Establish clear boundaries between work and personal life to prevent work from encroaching on your leisure time. Set

specific work hours and designate time for relaxation, hobbies, and time spent with loved ones.

2. **Unplug from technology:** Limit your use of electronic devices, such as smartphones and laptops, outside of work hours. Create tech-free zones or set boundaries around checking work emails and messages to prevent constant connectivity and promote work-life balance.

3. **Make time for self-care:** Prioritize self-care activities that nourish your body, mind, and soul. Make time for exercise, hobbies, relaxation, and socializing to recharge and rejuvenate outside of work.

4. **Practice assertiveness:** Learn to assertively communicate your needs and boundaries to colleagues, supervisors, and family members. Be

willing to say no to additional work or commitments that interfere with your work-life balance.

5. **Foster social connections:** invest time and energy into building and maintaining meaningful relationships with friends, family members, and colleagues. Social connections provide support, companionship, and a sense of belonging outside of work.

6. **Pursue passions and interests:** Make time for activities and hobbies that bring you joy and fulfillment. Whether it's painting, gardening, playing music, or volunteering, engaging in activities you love outside of work can enhance your overall well-being and satisfaction.

- **Schedule regular "me time":** Set aside dedicated time each week for self-care activities that rejuvenate and energize you, such as taking a long bath, reading a book, or practicing yoga.

- **Communicate openly:** Talk to your supervisor or manager about your need for work-life balance and explore flexible work arrangements or time-off options that accommodate your needs.

- **Seek support:** Don't hesitate to seek support from colleagues, friends, or a therapist if you're struggling to find balance or manage work-related stress. Sometimes, talking to someone can provide valuable perspective and support.

- The National Alliance on Mental Illness (NAMI) provides resources and support for individuals experiencing work-related stress or struggling to achieve work-life balance.

- The Mindful Workplace offers resources and programs for incorporating mindfulness and stress reduction techniques into the workplace to promote well-being and productivity.

- **Time Management Apps:** Explore apps such as Todoist, Trello, or Forest that can help you organize your tasks, prioritize your time, and maintain a healthy work-life balance.

Remember that finding balance between work and life is an ongoing process that requires self-awareness, intentionality, and adaptability. By prioritizing self-care, setting boundaries, and fostering social connections, you can create a healthier and more fulfilling balance between your professional and personal lives.

Chapter 14

Mindfulness in Daily Living

In our fast-paced world, cultivating mindfulness in daily life can bring a sense of calm, clarity, and presence to our experiences. In this chapter, we'll explore ways to integrate mindfulness into everyday activities, practice gratitude, and live in the present moment.

Integrating mindfulness into everyday activities

1. **Mindful breathing:** Take moments throughout the day to focus on your breath. Notice the sensation of air entering and leaving your nostrils or the rise and fall of your chest. Mindful breathing can help anchor you to the present moment and calm your mind during hectic times.

2. **Mindful eating:** Slow down and savor each bite of your meals. Pay attention to the flavors, textures, and sensations of the food as you eat. Notice the colors, smells, and sounds around you. Eating mindfully can enhance your enjoyment of food and promote healthy digestion.

3. **Mindful walking:** Take a break from your desk or daily routine to go for a mindful walk. Notice the sensation of your feet making contact with the ground, the rhythm of your steps, and the sights and sounds of your surroundings. Walking mindfully can help clear your mind and rejuvenate your body.

4. **Mindful listening:** Practice active listening during conversations with others. Focus your attention fully on the speaker without interrupting or

formulating your response in your mind. Listen with curiosity and empathy, and notice the nuances of tone, body language, and emotions conveyed through their words.

5. **Mindful work:** Bring mindfulness to your work tasks by focusing on one task at a time and giving it your full attention. Minimize distractions and resist the urge to multitask. Approach each task with a beginner's mind, noticing the details and nuances you may have overlooked before.

Practicing gratitude and living in the present moment

1. **Gratitude journaling:** Take a few minutes each day to write down three things you're grateful for. Focus on specific moments, experiences, or people that brought joy, comfort, or

meaning to your life. Cultivating gratitude can shift your perspective toward positivity and abundance.

2. **Mindful self-compassion:** Treat yourself with kindness and compassion, especially during challenging times. Notice self-critical thoughts or judgments and gently redirect them with self-compassionate statements. Practice self-care activities that nourish your body, mind, and soul.

3. **Embracing impermanence:** recognize the impermanent nature of life and appreciate each moment as it unfolds. Let go of attachments to outcomes or expectations and accept things as they are. Embracing impermanence can foster a sense of freedom and ease in the present moment.

4. **Mindful technology use:** Set boundaries around your use of technology and practice mindful awareness when engaging with screens. Notice how technology affects your mood, energy levels, and relationships, and make conscious choices about when and how to use it mindfully.

5. **Mindful rest:** Prioritize rest and relaxation as essential components of your daily routine. Set aside time each day for activities that recharge your body and mind, such as meditation, yoga, reading, or spending time in nature. Allow yourself to fully rest and rejuvenate without guilt or judgment.

Practical Tips for Cultivating Mindfulness

- **Start small:** Begin with short, simple mindfulness practices that you can easily integrate into your daily routine, such as mindful breathing or eating.

- **Be patient:** Cultivating mindfulness is a gradual process that takes time and practice. Be patient with yourself, and approach each moment with openness and curiosity.

- **Practice self-compassion:** Treat yourself with kindness and understanding, especially when you find it challenging to stay present or maintain mindfulness. Remember that mindfulness is about being present with whatever arises, without judgment or criticism.

- **Seek support:** Connect with mindfulness communities, classes, or teachers who can offer guidance, encouragement, and support on your mindfulness journey.

Resources for Further Exploration

- **Insight Timer**: Offers a wide range of guided meditations, mindfulness practices, and courses led by experienced teachers.
- The Power of Now by Eckhart Tolle explores the concept of living in the present moment and offers practical guidance for cultivating mindfulness in daily life.
- Mindful.org provides articles, guided meditations, and resources for integrating mindfulness into everyday activities and fostering a more mindful way of living.

By integrating mindfulness into your daily life and practicing gratitude and presence, you can cultivate a deeper sense of peace, fulfillment, and well-being. Remember that mindfulness is not about achieving a particular state of mind but about being fully present and engaged with each moment as it arises.

Chapter 15

Sustaining Mental Wellness

Maintaining mental health and wellness is an ongoing journey that requires consistent effort and attention. In this final chapter, we'll explore long-term strategies for sustaining mental wellness and creating a personalized self-care plan for ongoing well-being.

Long-Term Strategies for Maintaining Mental Health and Wellness

1. **Prioritize self-care:** Make self-care a non-negotiable part of your daily routine. Dedicate time each day for activities that nourish your body, mind, and soul, such as exercise, relaxation, hobbies, and socializing.

2. **Cultivate resilience:** Build resilience by developing coping skills, fostering social connections, and practicing

self-compassion. Embrace challenges as opportunities for growth and learning, and cultivate a positive mindset that helps you bounce back from setbacks.

3. **Stay connected:** Nurture supportive relationships with friends, family members, and community members. Stay connected with others through regular communication, shared activities, and acts of kindness. Social support is a vital buffer against stress and adversity.

4. **Manage stress effectively:** Develop healthy coping strategies for managing stress and preventing burnout. Practice relaxation techniques, such as deep breathing, meditation, or progressive muscle relaxation, and prioritize activities that help you unwind and recharge.

5. **Set realistic goals:** Set achievable goals that align with your values, interests, and priorities. Break larger goals into smaller, manageable steps, and celebrate your progress along the way. Setting and achieving goals can boost self-esteem and enhance overall well-being.

6. **Maintain a healthy lifestyle:** prioritize nutrition, exercise, sleep, and other lifestyle factors that contribute to overall health and well-being. Eat a balanced diet, engage in regular physical activity, prioritize sleep hygiene, and avoid harmful substances such as drugs and alcohol.

Creating a Personalized Self-Care Plan for Ongoing Well-Being

1. **Assess your needs**: Take inventory of your physical, emotional, and social

needs, as well as any challenges or stressors you may be facing. Identify areas where you could use additional support or resources to enhance your well-being.

2. **Identify self-care activities:** Brainstorm a list of self-care activities that resonate with you and address your needs and preferences. Consider activities that nourish your body (e.g., exercise, healthy eating), mind (e.g., meditation, journaling), and spirit (e.g., spending time in nature, practicing gratitude).

3. **Schedule self-care time:** Block out dedicated time in your schedule for self-care activities, just as you would for work or other commitments. Treat self-care as a priority rather than an afterthought, and honor your self-care time as sacred and non-negotiable.

4. **Be flexible and adaptive:** Be willing to adjust your self-care plan as needed based on changes in your circumstances or priorities. Be gentle with yourself and allow for flexibility and adaptability in your self-care routine.

5. **Practice self-compassion:** Approach self-care with an attitude of kindness, acceptance, and non-judgment. Be compassionate toward yourself, especially during times of stress or difficulty, and prioritize self-care as an act of self-love and self-preservation.

6. **Seek support:** Don't hesitate to reach out for support from friends, family members, or mental health professionals if you're struggling to maintain your mental wellness or adhere to your self-care plan.

Remember that it's okay to ask for help and that support is available to you.

Practical Tips for Sustaining Mental Wellness

- **Keep a self-care journal:** Use a journal to track your self-care activities, thoughts, and feelings and reflect on what brings you joy, fulfillment, and peace.

- **Create a supportive environment:** Surround yourself with people, places, and things that uplift and inspire you. Minimize exposure to negativity and stressors that drain your energy and affect your well-being.

- **Celebrate progress:** acknowledge and celebrate your achievements, no matter how small. Celebrating progress reinforces positive behaviors and motivates you to continue prioritizing your mental wellness.

Resources for Further Exploration

- The Five Dimensions of Well-Being by Tom Rath: Explores the interconnected dimensions of physical, emotional, social, financial, and community well-being and offers practical strategies for enhancing overall wellness.

- The Wellness Recovery Action Plan (WRAP) provides a structured framework for developing personalized wellness plans and strategies for managing mental health challenges and maintaining wellness.

- Local mental health resources: Explore local support groups, counseling services, wellness centers, or community organizations that offer resources and support for sustaining mental wellness.

Remember that sustaining mental wellness is an ongoing journey that requires commitment, self-awareness, and intentional action. By prioritizing self-care, fostering resilience, and seeking support when needed, you can cultivate a life of greater balance, fulfillment, and well-being.

9 798327 016088